My First Transportation Books

SHIPS GO!

Alan Walker

TABLE OF CONTENTS

A Crabtree Seedlings Book

CRABTREE
Publishing Company
www.crabtreebooks.com

Ships

Cruise ships go to faraway places.

People take vacations
on cruise ships.

Cargo ships carry goods all over the world.

Cranes load the goods onto the cargo ships.

Icebreakers can push through thick sea ice.

Icebreakers clear the way
for other ships and boats.

An aircraft carrier
is a **military ship**.

Military planes take off from and land on aircraft carriers.

Ships are **built** to travel on the water.

A submarine can travel on or under the water!

Glossary

built (BILT): Built means made or put together.

cranes (KRANEZ): Cranes are machines that can lift heavy things.

cruise (KROOZ): A cruise is a vacation on a ship.

military ship (MIL-uh-ter-ee SHIP): A military ship is used by the armed forces.

Index

School-to-Home Support for Caregivers and Teachers

This book helps children grow by letting them practice reading. Here are a few guiding questions to help the reader build his or her comprehension skills. Possible answers appear here in red.

Before Reading

- **What do I think this book is about?** I think this book is about many kinds of ships. I think this book is about where a ship can take you.

- **What do I want to learn about this topic?** I want to learn how big is the biggest ship. I want to learn about taking a vacation on a cruise ship.

During Reading

- **I wonder why...** I wonder why cargo ships travel all over the world. I wonder why cranes are used to load goods on cargo ships.

- **What have I learned so far?** I have learned that families like to take vacations on cruise ships. I have learned that an aircraft carrier is a military ship.

After Reading

- **What details did I learn about this topic?** I have learned that ships are built to travel on the water. I have learned that military planes can take off from and land on aircraft carriers.

- **Read the book again and look for the glossary words.** I see the word *cranes* on page 8, and the words *military ship* on page 14. The other glossary words are found on pages 22 and 23.

Library and Archives Canada Cataloguing in Publication

Available at the Library and Archives Canada

Library of Congress Cataloging-in-Publication Data

Available at the Library of Congress

Crabtree Publishing Company

www.crabtreebooks.com   1–800–387–7650

Print book version produced jointly with Blue Door Education in 2023

Written by: Alan Walker

Print coordinator: Katherine Berti

Printed in the U.S.A./072022/CG20220201

PHOTO CREDITS:
Cover and Pages 2-3 © NAPA, page 4 © Brocreative, page 5 © photobeginner, pages 6-7 © Aun Photographer, pages 8-9 © MAGNIFIER, pages 10-11 © shmatkov, page 12 © itechno, page 13 © LuYago, Pages 14-15 © GreenOak, page 16 © AlejandroCarnicero, page 17 © GreenOak, pages 18-19 © Ezgi Erol, page 20 © Aerial-motion, page 21 © noraismail. All images from Shutterstock.com

Published in the United States
Crabtree Publishing
347 Fifth Ave.
Suite 1402-145
New York, NY 10016

Published in Canada
Crabtree Publishing
616 Welland Ave.
St. Catharines, Ontario
L2M 5V6